READY, SET, GAME!

CONSOLE GAMING

BY BETSY RATHBURN

TORQUE™

BELLWETHER MEDIA • MINNEAPOLIS, MN

TORQUE™

TORQUE brims with excitement perfect for thrill-seekers of all kinds. Discover daring survival skills, explore uncharted worlds, and marvel at mighty engines and extreme sports. In *Torque* books, anything can happen. Are you ready?

This edition first published in 2021 by Bellwether Media, Inc.

Library of Congress Cataloging-in-Publication Data

LC record for Console Gaming available at https://lccn.loc.gov/2020048063

Editor: Elizabeth Neuenfeldt   Designer: Brittany McIntosh

Printed in the United States of America, North Mankato, MN.

TABLE OF CONTENTS

CHAMPION!

Time to play *Super Smash Bros. Ultimate*! You choose to play as Yoshi. You play against Link and Kirby. Who will win?

As the battle rages, Kirby knocks Link out with his mallet. Then Kirby flies toward you. But you launch an egg just in time. Kirby is defeated. Yoshi is the champion!

CONSOLE GAMING HISTORY

The first in-home gaming console came out in 1972. It was called the Magnavox Odyssey.

This console was very simple. It had plastic **overlays** that went on the TV screen. Overlays showed maps, mazes, and grids. Players used controllers to move lights behind the overlays. Players had to track their own scores!

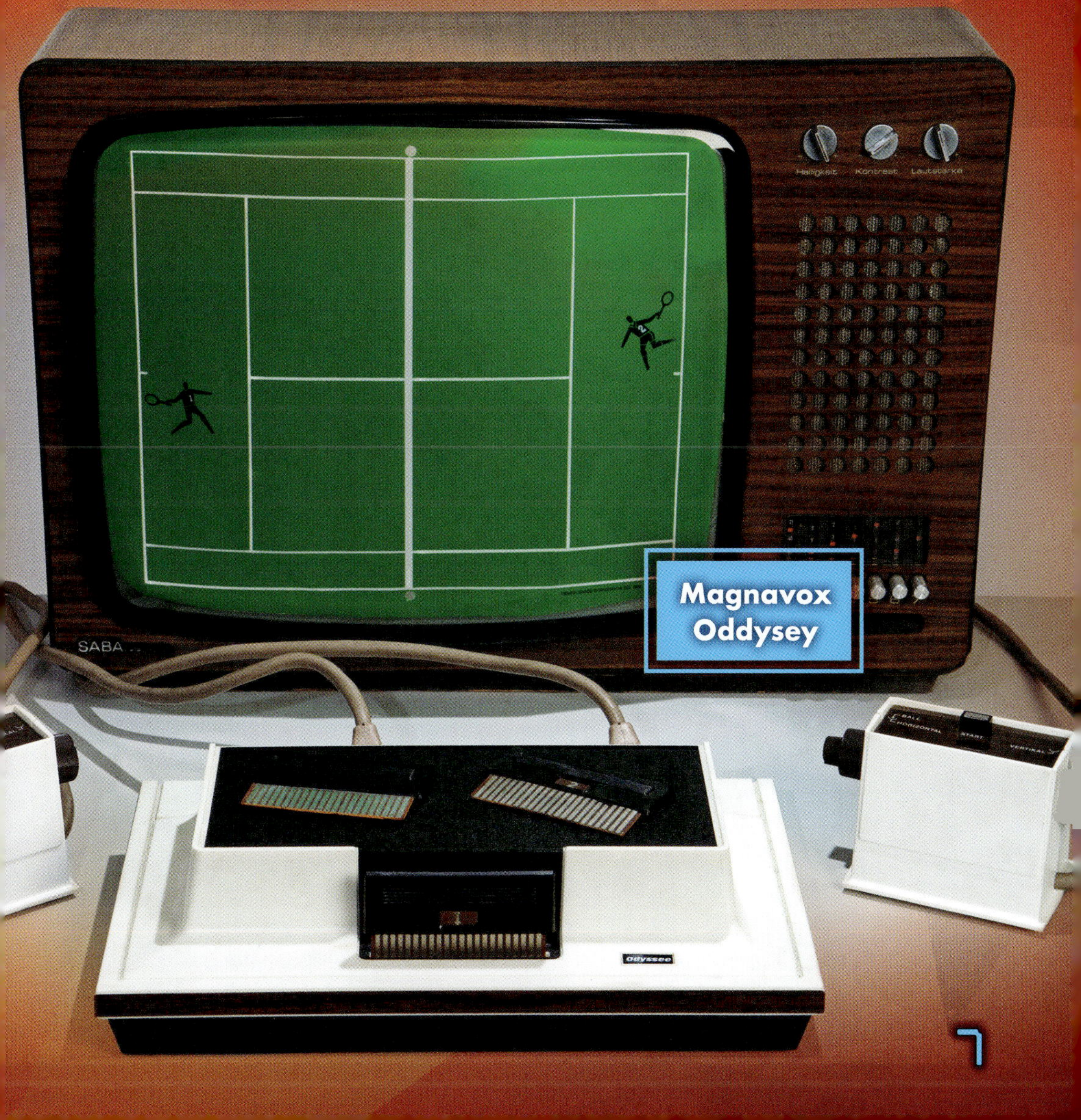

Magnavox Oddysey

CONSOLE GAMING TIMELINE

1972

Magnavox Odyssey is released

1975

Atari *Pong* is released for home consoles

1976

The Fairchild Channel F is released

1983

Sega SG-1000 is released

1983

NES is released in Japan as the Famicom

1988

Sega Genesis is first released in Japan as the Mega Drive

1990

SNES is first released in Japan as the Super Famicom

1994

Sega Saturn and Sony PlayStation are released

1996

Nintendo 64 is released

Pong

Soon, more consoles were made. Atari released *Pong* on home consoles in 1975. It was the first console game with sound!

A year later, Jerry Lawson created the Fairchild Channel F. It was the first console with **microprocessors**. These tiny computers brought more power to console gaming. They led to better **graphics** and games!

WHAT'S THE NAME?

Early Nintendo and Sega consoles were first released in Japan. They often had different names. The NES and SNES were called the Famicom and Super Famicom. The Sega Genesis was called the Mega Drive!

game cartridges

The Fairchild Channel F was also the first console to use **cartridges**. Before, all games were stored on consoles. Other companies quickly made cartridge consoles.

Fairchild Channel F

In 1983, the Nintendo Entertainment System (NES) and the Sega SG-1000 came out in Japan. A **rivalry** had begun! Sega introduced the Sega Genesis in 1988. Later, Nintendo made the Super Nintendo Entertainment System (SNES).

Sega Genesis

POPULAR NINTENDO CONSOLE GAMES

(BY GAMES SOLD)

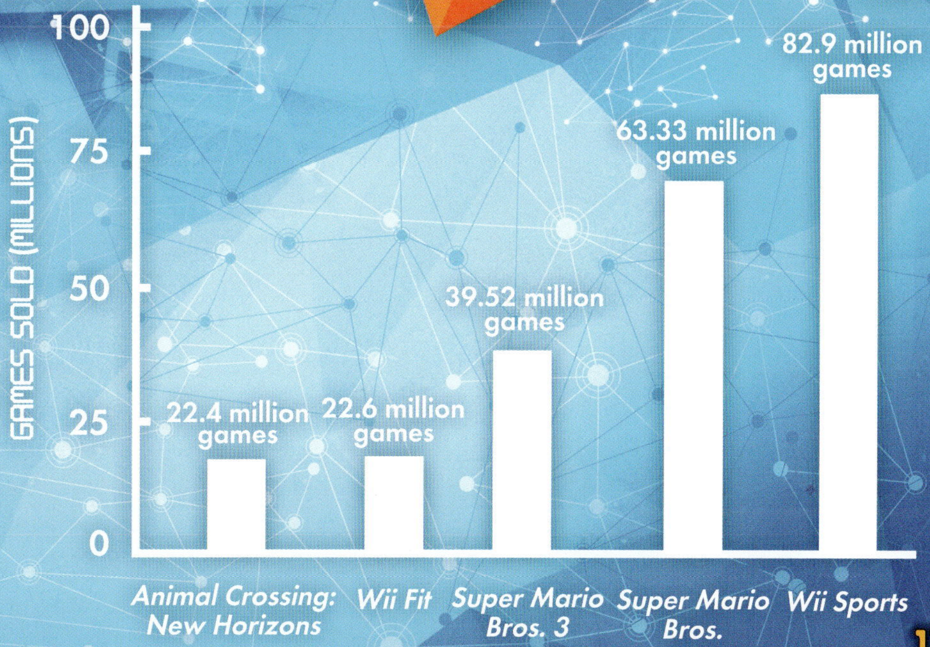

The rivalry continued in the 1990s. The Sega Saturn came out in 1994. It was among the first consoles to use CDs. In 1996, Nintendo made the Nintendo 64. *Super Mario 64* was its best-selling game!

Nintendo 64

Super Mario 64

Sony started making consoles, too. They released the PlayStation in 1994. Games such as *Crash Bandicoot* and *Spyro the Dragon* made it a hit!

Spyro the Dragon

SKATE SKILLS

Sports games were popular on the PlayStation. In 1999, *Tony Hawk's Pro Skater* was released. It was very popular. In 2020, the game was remade with better graphics!

Tony Hawk's Pro Skater 1+2

CONSOLE GAMING TODAY

Sega no longer makes new consoles. But Nintendo and Sony still make them. Their consoles include 2017's Nintendo Switch and 2020's PlayStation 5.

The Xbox is also popular. It was first introduced in 2001. In 2020, the Xbox Series X was released. The Xbox Series S was released at the same time.

CONSOLES THROUGH TIME

NINTENDO

1983
NES

1990
SNES

1996
Nintendo 64

2001
GameCube

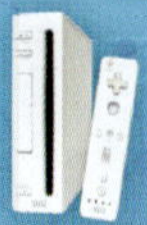
2006
Wii

2012
Wii U

2017
Nintendo Switch

SONY

1994
PlayStation

2000
PlayStation 2

2006
PlayStation 3

2013
PlayStation 4

2020
PlayStation 5

MICROSOFT

2001
Xbox

2005
Xbox 360

2013
Xbox One

2016
Xbox One S

2017
Xbox One X

2020
Xbox Series X

2020
Xbox Series S

Animal Crossing: New Horizons

Rocket League

Newer consoles have improved graphics and **memory**. Online gameplay is common, too. Players can play online with people around the world! They may battle in *Rocket League* or trade items in *Animal Crossing: New Horizons*.

People also play **virtual reality** games on consoles. The PlayStation VR includes a **headset**. It makes games feel like you are in them!

PlayStation VR

GAME SPOTLIGHT

GAME *Fall Guys: Ultimate Knockout*

YEAR 2020

CONSOLE PlayStation 4

TYPE action, battle royale

DESCRIPTION Up to 60 players compete online in challenges to qualify for each round. The player who wins the final round is the champion!

THE CONSOLE GAMING COMMUNITY

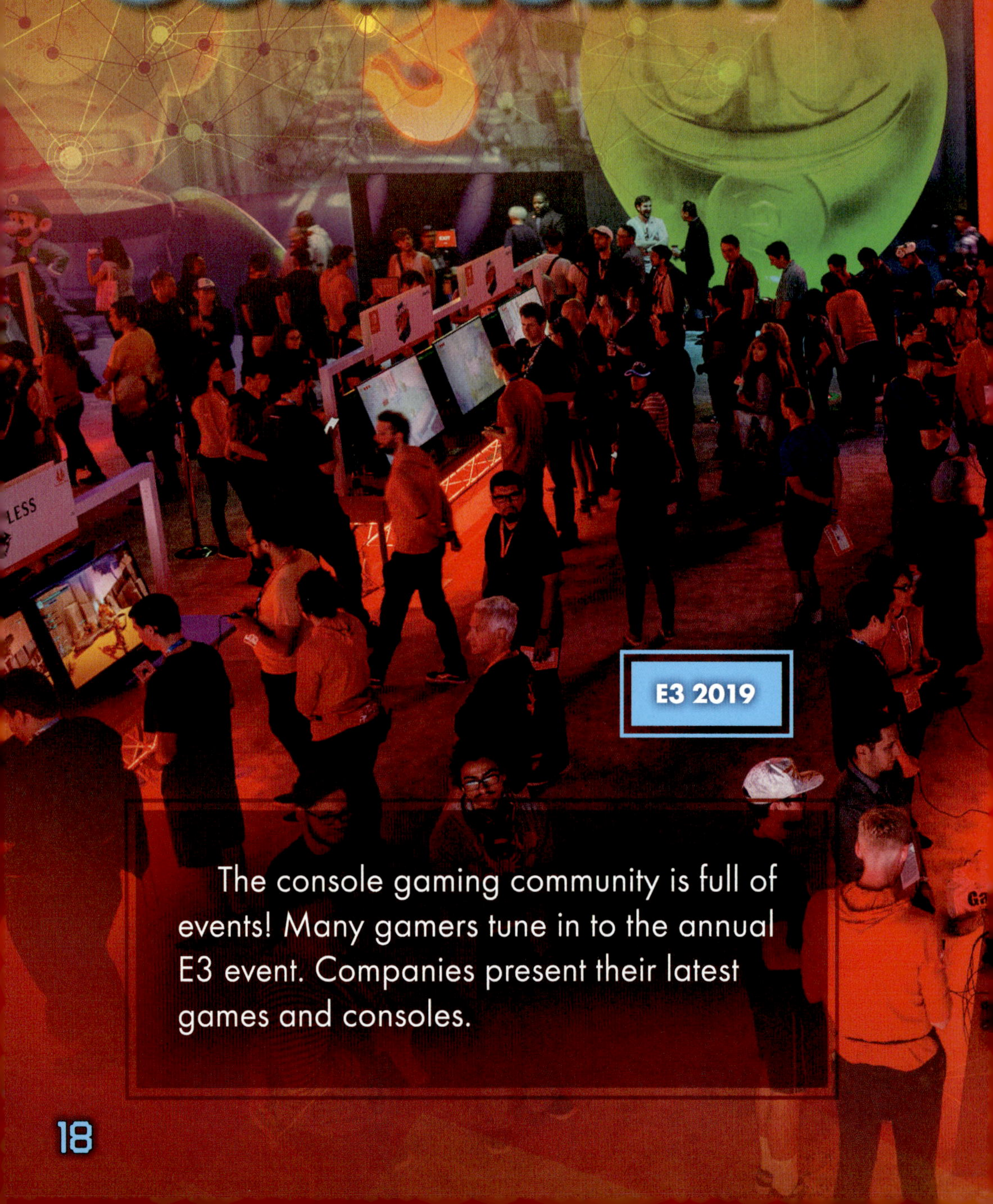

E3 2019

The console gaming community is full of events! Many gamers tune in to the annual E3 event. Companies present their latest games and consoles.

Dragon Ball FighterZ

Competitions also bring gamers together. Many **tournaments** are held each year. In 2019, the first *Dragon Ball FighterZ* world tour was held. Players competed to become the champion of this popular fighting game!

Some gaming competitions are for **charity**. Games Done Quick is a **speedrunning** competition. It happens twice a year. Gamers race to finish games in the fastest time possible. Since 2010, the event has raised more than $28 million!

CONSOLE GAMING EVENT SPOTLIGHT

EVENTS Summer Games Done Quick and Awesome Games Done Quick

PURPOSE Players speedrun popular games to raise money for charity

YEAR FIRST HELD 2010

WHEN IT HAPPENS twice per year

TOTAL MONEY RAISED more than $28 million

Console gaming will continue to be popular. People can play alone, or with friends around the world!

Summer Games Done Quick

GLOSSARY

cartridges—devices that hold memory and graphics for games; cartridges are inserted into consoles.

charity—aid given to those in need

competitions—events in which people are trying to win the same thing

graphics—images displayed on a computer screen

headset—a helmet, visor, or other item that a person wears on their head to experience virtual reality

memory—the ability to store information

microprocessors—small chips that hold a computer's memory

overlays—clear, plastic sheets with designs that were placed over television screens so that people could play the Magnavox Odyssey

rivalry—a long-standing competition between two sides

speedrunning—the act of completing a game as quickly as possible

tournaments—series of contests or games that make up competitions

virtual reality—related to games that allow players to explore a human-made setting

TO LEARN MORE

AT THE LIBRARY

Gregory, Josh. *History of Esports.* Ann Arbor, Mich.: Cherry Lake Publishing, 2020.

Hansen, Dustin. *Game On!: Video Game History from Pong and Pac-Man to Mario, Minecraft, and More.* New York, N.Y.: Feiwel & Friends, 2016.

Rathburn, Betsy. *Computer Gaming.* Minneapolis, Minn.: Bellwether Media, 2021.

ON THE WEB

FACTSURFER

Factsurfer.com gives you a safe, fun way to find more information.

1. Go to www.factsurfer.com.

2. Enter "console gaming" into the search box and click 🔍.

3. Select your book cover to see a list of related content.

INDEX

The images in this book are reproduced through the courtesy of: v74, front cover (Wii); Anthony McLaughlin, front cover (Xbox One); robtek, front cover (PS2), pp. 8 (NES), 10 (top), 11, 12 (top), 15 (NES, SNES, Nintendo 64, GameCube), 15 (PS2); *Super Smash Bros. Ultimate*/ Bellwether Media, pp. 4, 5 (top, bottom); SenseiAlan/ Flickr, p. 6; INTERFOTO/ Alamy, pp. 7, 9; Evan-Amos/ Wikipedia, pp. 8 (Magnavox Odyssey), Idealink Photography/ Alamy, p. 8 (Atari *Pong*); Matthieu Tuffet, p. 8 (SNES); *Super Mario 64*/ Andy Robinson, p. 12 (bottom); Activision/ Wikipedia, p. 13 (top); *Tony Hawk's Pro Skater 1+2*/ Sony, p. 13 (bottom); Paul Stringer, p. 14 (Switch); DecaStock/ Alamy, p. 14 (PS5); Xbox Wire/ Xbox Media Kit, pp. 14 (Xbox Series S and Series X), 15 (Xbox 360, Xbox One, Xbox One S, Xbox One X, Xbox Series X, Xbox Series S); seeshooteatrepeat, p. 15 (Wii); Interneteable, p. 15 (Wii U); Matt Skills, p. 15 (Switch); JR Moreira, p. 15 (PlayStation); Tony Cordoza/ Alamy, p. 15 (PS3); Peter Kotoff, p. 15 (PS4); Aldeca Productions, p. 15 (PS5); julie deshaies, p. 15 (Xbox); *Animal Crossing: New Horizons*/ Bellwether Media, p. 16 (top); *Rocket League*/ Epic Games, p. 16 (bottom); Aleksandra Suzi/ Alamy, p. 17 (top); *Fall Guys: Ultimate Knockout*/ Mediatonic, p. 17 (bottom); Xinhua/ Alamy, pp. 18-19; *Dragon Ball FighterZ*/ Arc System Works, p. 19; Gage Skidmore/ Flickr, pp. 20-21.